Overview *A World of Masks*

Children learn about masks and how to make one.

Reading Vocabulary Words

festivals
gold
carved

High-Frequency Words

some	watch
old	happy
bear	made
dry	wood

Building Future Vocabulary

* *These vocabulary words do not appear in this text. They are provided to develop related oral vocabulary that first appears in future texts.*

Words:	shape	disguise	touch
Levels:	Silver	Gold	Gold

Comprehension Strategy
Building background knowledge

Fluency Skill
Reading exclamatory sentences in an excited manner

Phonics Skill
Using knowledge of vowel diphthong /oi/ (b<u>oy</u>)

Reading-Writing Connection
Making a list

Home Connection
Send home one of the Flying Colors Take-Home books for children to share with their families.

Differentiated Instruction
Before reading the text, query children to discover their level of understanding of the comprehension strategy — Building background knowledge. As you work together, provide additional support to children who show a beginning mastery of the strategy.

Focus on ELL
- Have children look at the pictures of masks in the book.

- Ask children to draw a picture of a mask they have seen. Encourage them to discuss when and where they saw the mask.

T1

Using This Teaching Version

1. Before Reading
2. During Reading
3. Revisiting the Text
4. Assessment

This Teaching Version will assist you in directing children through the process of reading.

1. **Begin with Before Reading** to familiarize children with the book's content. Select the skills and strategies that meet the needs of your children.

2. **Next, go to During Reading** to help children become familiar with the text, and then to read individually on their own.

3. **Then, go back to Revisiting the Text** and select those specific activities that meet children's needs.

4. **Finally, finish with Assessment** to confirm children are ready to move forward to the next text.

1 Before Reading

Building Background

- Write the word *festivals* on the board. Read it aloud. Ask *What are festivals?* (fairs, carnivals, parties, events) Have children share what they know about festivals. Ask children about any festivals they may have attended.

- Introduce the book by reading the title, talking about the cover photograph, and sharing the overview.

Building Future Vocabulary
Use Interactive Modeling Card: Word Log

- Introduce the words *shape*, *disguise*, and *touch* by writing them on the Word Log.

- Have children look up each word in a dictionary. Record definitions on the Word Log and discuss how each word may relate to *A World of Masks*.

Introduction to Reading Vocabulary

- On blank cards write: *festivals*, *gold*, and *carved*. Read them aloud. Tell children these words will appear in the text of *A World of Masks*.

- Use each word in a sentence for understanding.

Introduction to Comprehension Strategy

Use Interactive Modeling Card: Nonfiction Questions and Answers

- Explain that building background knowledge means learning new things to help us understand what we read.
- Ask children what they know and want to learn about masks. List their responses in the appropriate columns of the Nonfiction Questions and Answers chart.
- Tell children to keep these questions in mind as they read *A World of Masks*.

Introduction to Phonics

- Write *boy* on the board. Read the word aloud. Ask *What word rhymes with **boy** and is something to play with?* (**toy**) Write **toy** on the board. Underline *oy* in both words.
- Explain that /oi/ can come at the beginning, middle, or end of a word. Ask *What sound does a pig make?* (**oink**) *What are pennies, nickels, dimes, and quarters?* (**coins**)
- Have children look for words with dipthong /oi/ as they read *A World of Masks*.

Modeling Fluency

- Tell the children you are going to read a passage twice. Then read aloud the text box on page 5 without any expression. When you read it again, emphasize enthusiasm and excitement in the second sentence. Ask *Which way did you prefer hearing this passage read? Why?*
- Explain that exclamation points are used to identify excitement in a surprising fact or dramatic story.

2 During Reading

Book Talk

Beginning on page T4, use the During Reading notes on the left-hand side to engage children in a book talk. On page 24, follow with Individual Reading.

During Reading

Book Talk
- Discuss the cover photograph. Ask *Who do you think made these masks?* (the children)
- Discuss how to use a table of contents. Ask *Where in the book would you look to find out about masks worn during festivals?* (Chapter 3, pages 6 and 7)

➤ *Turn to page 2 – Book Talk*

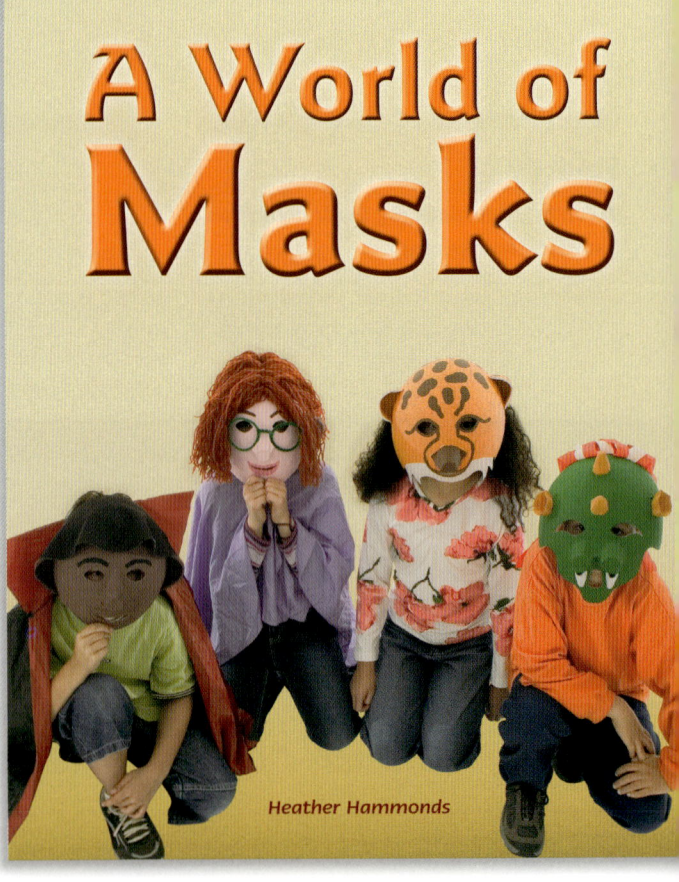

Revisiting the Text

A World of Masks

Heather Hammonds

Chapter 1	Masks	2
Chapter 2	Stories and Plays	4
Chapter 3	Festival Fun	6
Chapter 4	Masks of Long Ago	8
Chapter 5	Making Masks	10
Chapter 6	Make Your Own Mask	12
Chapter 7	Fun with Your Mask	22
Glossary and Index		24

Future Vocabulary
- Ask *What is a disguise?* (costume, mask, dressing up so people don't recognize you) *Can a mask be a disguise?* (yes) Explain that *disguise* can be a noun or a verb.

During Reading

Book Talk

- Point out the symbols next to the chapter title. Ask children to describe them. (happy mask and sad mask)
- Point out that the words on page 3 are in three different gold boxes. Have children follow along with their fingers as you read the page aloud.
- **Comprehension Strategy** Remind children that they can use what they already know about masks to help them understand what they read in *A World of Masks*. Encourage children to add new questions to the Nonfiction Questions and Answers chart.

Turn to page 4 — Book Talk

Chapter 1

Masks

Have you ever put on a **mask**? When you wear a mask, you can look like someone or something else.

Revisiting the Text

There are lots of masks from all around the world.

Some masks look like people or animals.

Some masks have lots of **decorations**.

Future Vocabulary

- Compare and contrast the children's masks on page 2 with the masks on page 3. Ask *How are the masks alike?* (They all cover the face.) *How are the masks different?* (Some are scary; some are people and some are animals; they are made with different materials.)

- Continue your discussion of disguises using these masks as examples. Have children discuss a time when they wore a disguise, such as in a play, at a party, or while playing dress up. Have children use the word *disguise* in a sentence.

Now revisit pages 4–5

During Reading

Book Talk
- Ask a volunteer to read the chapter title aloud. Have children name one of their favorite stories and tell what mask they would wear if they were telling the story to the class. Ask *Do you think wearing a mask when you tell a story is a good idea? Why?* (Yes, it is more fun. No, it is harder to speak wearing a mask.)

- **Fluency Skill** Point to the text box on page 5. Ask *What is the punctuation mark at the end of the second sentence?* (exclamation point) *What does that tell us?* (to read in an excited manner) Ask a volunteer to read the text box on page 5 with enthusiasm.

Turn to page 6 – Book Talk

Chapter 2
Stories and Plays

Sometimes people wear masks when they tell a story or act in a play.

This mask is used to tell a very old story about a bear.

a mask from Alaska

4

4

Revisiting the Text

The man in this play is telling a story from Japan.

This person is telling a story about sharks. Look at the big teeth!

Future Vocabulary
- Have children name familiar *shape*s. (square, circle, triangle) Ask *What shapes do you see on these masks?* (triangles for the teeth and the shark's jaw; ovals for the eyes) Refer back to the Word Log. Have children confirm their definition for *shape*.

Now revisit pages 6–7

5

During Reading

Book Talk

- Have children locate the word *festivals* on page 6. Say *Festivals is in boldfaced type. What does that tell us?* (The word *festivals* is in the glossary; it is an important word in this book.) Discuss *festivals* with children. Ask *What would you expect to see at a festival?* (a parade, costumes, dancing, people wearing masks) Have volunteers describe something they have seen at a *festival*.

Turn to page 8 – Book Talk

Chapter 3  **Festival Fun**

In some places, masks are worn at special **festivals**.

At the festivals, there are big **parades**. People dress up in **costumes** and put on their masks.

6

Revisiting the Text

Lots of people come to watch the parades. Festivals are a lot of fun.

Future Vocabulary

- Ask *Can you tell what these people look like under their masks?* (no) *They are in disguise.* Have children talk about how they would *disguise* themselves to hide who they are. Have them use *disguise* in a sentence that describes what they would look like, such as *I would disguise myself as a cat.*

- Say *People can disguise what they look like. They can also disguise how they feel.* Discuss how and why people would want to *disguise* how they feel. Add this new meaning to the Word Log.

Now revisit pages 8–9

During Reading

Book Talk

- Have children locate the word *gold* on page 9. Say *The word gold is also in boldfaced type. What does that tell us?* (*Gold* is in the glossary.) *Where is the glossary?* (at the back of the book) With children, turn to page 24 and read the glossary definition for *gold*.

- Say *The masks on page 9 are made with gold. What else is made with gold?* (jewelry) Discuss alternate meanings for *gold*. Say *Gold is a metal. Gold is also a color.* Have children make up sentences with *gold*, using either meaning of the word.

- Have children point to the captions on page 8. Remind them that as they read, they should remember to read captions.

Turn to page 10 – Book Talk

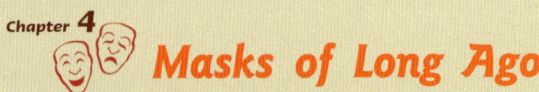

Chapter 4

Masks of Long Ago

Some masks are very old.

Long ago, people wore these masks in special plays about sad things and happy things.

a sad mask

a happy mask

very old masks from Greece

8

Revisiting the Text

This very old mask is made of **gold**.

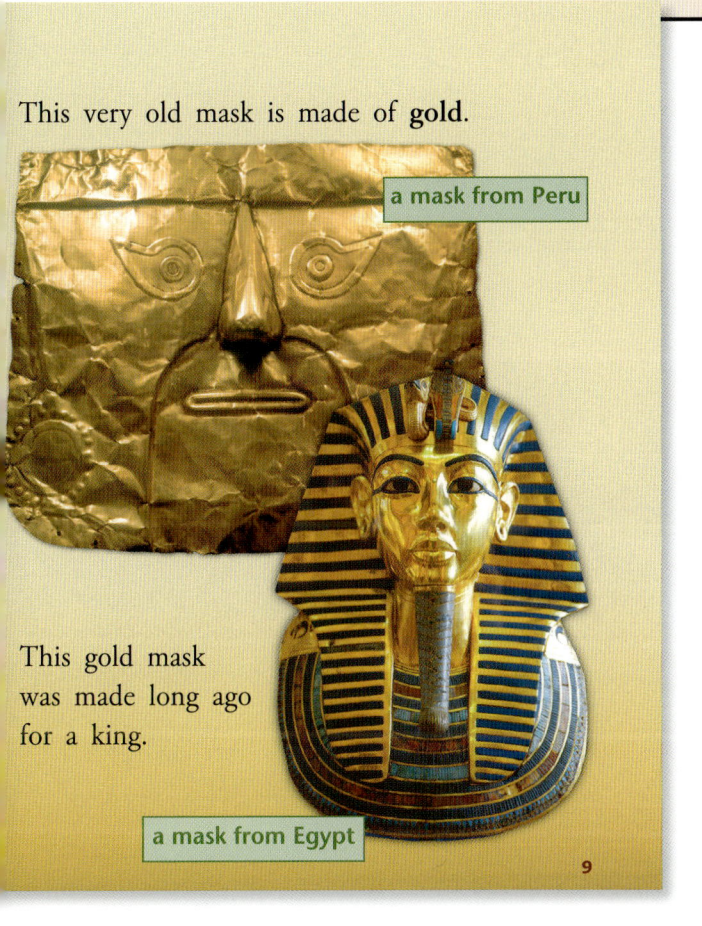

a mask from Peru

This gold mask was made long ago for a king.

a mask from Egypt

Future Vocabulary
- Ask *How do you think people shape gold into masks?* (They flatten it with a hammer.) *How do people shape clay?* (with their hands, with tools, on a potter's wheel) Discuss how *shape* as a verb is different from *shape* as a noun.

Now revisit pages 10–11

During Reading

Book Talk

- Have children locate the word *carved* on page 10. Say *Carved is also in boldfaced type. What do you know about such words?* (They are in the glossary.) Have children look up *carved* in the glossary and read the definition together.

- Say *The masks on page 10 are carved out of wood. What other things can we carve?* (meat, stone, clay)

- Have children locate something made of *gold* in the picture on page 11. (man's ring and watch)

Turn to page 12 — Book Talk

Chapter 5

Making Masks

Masks can be made in many ways.

Some masks are made of wood. They are **carved** with special tools.

10

Revisiting the Text

Masks are also made by putting **plaster** or paper into a **mold**.

Masks can be painted. Jewels and other decorations are put on them, too.

Future Vocabulary

- Discuss what the people in these pictures are *touch*ing. Ask *What do these masks feel like to the touch?* (smooth) *What does the plaster feel like to the touch?* (wet) With children, confirm the definition for *touch* they wrote in the Word Log earlier in the lesson. Modify if necessary.

Now revisit pages 12–13

During Reading

Book Talk

- **Phonics Skill** Read page 12 aloud. Have children raise their hands when they hear a word with /oi/. *(boy)* Ask *What is another word for* happiness *that rhymes with* boy? *(joy)* Write *joy* on the board and underline *oy*.

- Have a volunteer read the chapter title aloud. Point out the list on page 12 and the supplies on page 13. Ask *How do you think this chapter is different from the earlier chapters?* (Earlier chapters described kinds of masks, and this chapter will tell how to make masks.)

Turn to page 14 — Book Talk

12

Revisiting the Text

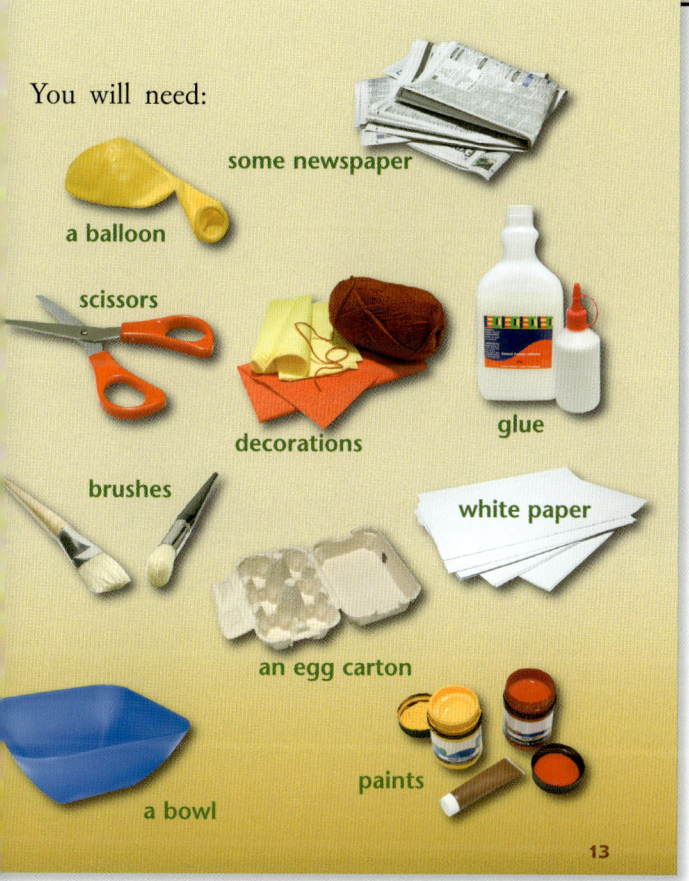

Future Vocabulary
- Discuss the *shape*s of the materials in the picture on page 13. Ask *What shape is the white paper?* (a rectangle) *What shape is the lid for the paints?* (a circle) *Do you think the mask is shaping up nicely, or does it need a few final touches?* Have children find other *shape*s in the classroom.

Now revisit pages 14–15

13

During Reading

Book Talk

- Ask *Are they making a carved mask?* (no) *Are they making a mask out of gold?* (no) *What are their supplies?* (balloons and newspaper)

- **Phonics Skill** Ask *If you wanted to make a mask that looked like it was made of silver, what could you use?* (aluminum foil) If children do not think of aluminum foil, prompt them with questions, such as *What is shiny and thin like a sheet of paper?* After someone suggests foil, say *The word* foil *has /oi/, too. Is that sound at the beginning, middle, or end of the word?* (middle)

Turn to page 16 – Book Talk

Revisiting the Text

- Stick the newspaper onto the balloon. Leave some of the balloon showing at the end.
- Let the newspaper dry.

Future Vocabulary
- Ask *What are the girls touching in these pictures?* (balloon, newspaper, scissors) Discuss alternate meanings for *touch*. Ask *What does it mean to keep in touch with someone?* (talk or write to them regularly) *What do we mean when we say something, such as a movie or photograph, is touching?* (It makes us feel an emotion, such as joy or sadness.) *What does it mean to have a touch of the flu?* (a mild case) Space permitting, add these meanings to the Word Log.

Now revisit pages 16–17

During Reading

Book Talk

- Ask *Why don't the girls use gold to make their mask?* (It is expensive.) Explain that gold is a very soft metal. Discuss gold leaf, and explain that it is not called *leaf* because it is part of a tree. Gold leaf is what you get when you hammer gold until it is as thin as a leaf. Explain that people sometimes use gold leaf to cover other metals to make them look like they are made from solid gold.

Turn to page 18 – Book Talk

⊕ Put some more glue and newspaper into the bowl.

⊕ Then stick the newspaper onto the balloon again.

⊕ Let the newspaper dry.

Revisiting the Text

- Stick some ears and a nose onto the balloon.
- Then cut the white paper into lots of little pieces.

Future Vocabulary
- Say *One of the girls is cutting paper into shapes.* Ask children if they have a favorite shape. *Do you like shapes with points, like stars, or smooth shapes, like circles?* Discuss how familiar shapes are alike and different (Rectangles and squares have four sides and right angles; triangles and stars both have points.)

Now revisit pages 18–19

During Reading

Book Talk

- Say *The girls are gluing paper onto a balloon to make a mask. Has anyone seen the huge balloons or masks at a Thanksgiving Day parade?* Discuss whether the Thanksgiving holiday is a festival. Have children share and support their ideas about what makes a celebration a festival. Have children complete this sentence stem about festivals: *A festival is _____.* (like a party, fun, a holiday)

- **Fluency Skill** Point to page 19. Ask *What is about to happen?* (The girls are going to cut the balloon.) *How can you tell this is an exciting moment?* (open mouths, colorful text design, exclamation point) Read the page together with excitement.

Turn to page 20 — Book Talk

- Put some glue and white paper into the bowl.
- Then stick the white paper onto the balloon.
- Let the paper dry.

18

Revisiting the Text

Now it is time to pop the balloon.

Future Vocabulary
- Ask *On which page do you see a star shape?* (page 19) *What word is inside this shape?* (pop)
- Ask *What does it mean if someone is in good shape?* (They are healthy or fit.) *How do we stay in shape?* (exercise, eat right) *Why is it important to stay in good shape?* (so that our bodies are healthy)

Now revisit pages 20–21

During Reading

Book Talk
- Say *Now the girls are cutting into the mask. Why?* (so it can fit over the face)
- Ask *What are the girls using to cut their mask?* (scissors) Discuss scissor safety rules, such as *Do not run with scissors* and *Pass scissors carefully.* Have children predict what the girls will do next.

Turn to page 22 – Book Talk

⊕ Cut out some eyes and a mouth.
⊕ Cut around the end of the mask, too.

Revisiting the Text

🎨 Paint your mask.

🎨 When the paint is dry, stick some decorations on it.

Future Vocabulary
- **Phonics Skill** Say *The girls are painting their mask. Did you know that some paints are made with oil? Let's say* oil *together. What sound is at the beginning of* oil? *Add* oil *to the list of /oi/ words. Ask What word rhymes with* oil *and describes how we roll up rope or yarn? (coil) What other words rhyme with* oil *and* coil? *(boil, foil, soil)*

Now revisit pages 22–23

During Reading

Book Talk

- Leave this page spread for children to discover on their own when they read the book individually.

Turn to page 24 – Book Talk

Chapter 7

Fun with Your Mask

Put on your mask and have some fun.
You can act in a play.
You can tell a story.

Revisiting the Text

You can even march in a parade with your friends!

Future Vocabulary
- Ask a volunteer to read the chapter title aloud. Ask *Is it fun to wear a disguise?* (yes) *Why?* (We can be something or someone different; we can experience new things.)

Go to page T5 – Revisiting the Text

During Reading

Book Talk
* Note: Point out this text feature page as a reference point for children's usage while reading independently.

Individual Reading
Have each child read the entire book at his or her own pace while remaining in the group.

Go to page T5 – Revisiting the Text

Glossary

carved	cut out or shaped from wood or stone
costumes	clothes worn by people to make them look like someone or something else
decorations	things used to make something look good
festivals	big parties that often happen at the same time every year
gold	a shiny yellow metal
mask	something that is put on the face to change the way a person looks or keep them safe when they are playing sports
mold	something that gives shape to other things when they are pressed onto it or poured into it
parades	fun marches often held at festival time
plaster	a white powder that turns hard when it is mixed with water

Index

animals 3, 12
carving 10
costumes 6
decorations 3, 21
festivals 6–7
gold 9
making masks 10–21

mold 11
painting 11, 21
paper 11, 13–28
parades 6, 7, 23
plaster 11
plays 4, 8, 22
stories 4, 5, 22

24

During independent work time, children can read the online book at:
www.rigbyflyingcolors.com

24

Revisiting the Text

Future Vocabulary
- Use the notes on the right-hand pages to develop oral vocabulary that goes beyond the text. These vocabulary words first appear in future texts. These words are: *shape*, *disguise*, and *touch*.

Turn back to page 1

Reading Vocabulary Review
Activity Sheet: New Word Log

- Have children write *festivals*, *gold*, and *carved* in the New Word Log. Have them find the meaning in the text and explain why they think the author chose each word.
- Have children add other new words from *A World of Masks*.

Comprehension Strategy Review
Use Interactive Modeling Card: Nonfiction Questions and Answers

- Discuss *A World of Masks*. Review the questions children had before they read *A World of Masks*.
- With children, fill in the rest of the Nonfiction Question and Answers chart.

Phonics Review
- Review the list of /oi/ words. Say each word to make sure children recognize the vowel diphthong /oi/.
- Have children go on a word hunt for more /oi/ words in familiar texts. Add the words to the list.

Fluency Review
- Turn to pages 22–23. Partner children and have them take turns reading the exclamatory sentence in an excited manner.
- Have children take turns reading the sentences on page 22 again. Ask them to pretend that these three sentences also have exclamation points. Discuss how exclamation points change the way we think about what we read.

Reading-Writing Connection
Activity Sheet: Text Connections Web

To assist children with linking reading and writing:
- Model how to use the Text Connections Web. Then have children complete the Activity Sheet for *A World of Masks*.
- Have children use the completed Web to make a list of when and where they have worn masks or seen other people wearing masks.

T5

4 Assessment

Assessing Future Vocabulary

Work with each child individually. Ask questions that elicit each child's understanding of the Future Vocabulary words. Note each child's responses:

- If you shape wood, what are you doing?
- What would you wear to disguise yourself?
- Can you touch your toes?

Assessing Comprehension Strategy

Work with each child individually. Note each child's understanding of building background knowledge:

- Where would you expect to find someone wearing a mask?
- What are masks made from?
- Was each child able to build background knowledge to better understand *A World of Masks?*

Assessing Phonics

Work with each child individually. Say a series of words and have each child raise a hand whenever you say a word with /oi/. Note each child's responses for understanding the vowel diphthong /oi/:

- Use the following words: *boy, big, oil, toy, only, coin, tub,* and *foil.*
- Did each child raise his or her hand for every word with /oi/?

Assessing Fluency

Have each child read pages 22–23 to you. Note each child's understanding of reading exclamatory sentences in an excited manner:

- Was each child able to identify both the exclamation point and its purpose?
- Did each child read the exclamatory sentence with excitement?

Interactive Modeling Cards

Word Log

Title: *A World of Masks*

Word	Meaning from Selection
shape	a form or outline, such as a circle, square, or triangle
disguise	a costume or mask
touch	feeling something

Directions: With children, fill in the Word Log using the words *shape*, *disguise*, and *touch*.

Nonfiction Questions and Answers

	Before Reading		During Reading	After Reading
	What do I know about this topic?	What do I want to find out by reading this book?	What did I learn?	What new questions do I have?
	People wear masks over their faces. People wear masks to look like someone else.	How do people make masks? Where do people wear masks?	People make masks from gold. People use masks to tell stories.	What else can you use to make a mask? What is the most popular mask worn for Halloween?

Directions: With children, fill in the Nonfiction Questions and Answers chart for *A World of Masks*.

Discussion Questions

- What do some very old masks from Greece look like? (Literal)
- Why did the girls use the balloon to make their mask? (Critical Thinking)
- Why do some people wear masks when they tell stories? (Inferential)

T7

Activity Sheets

New Word Log

New Word	Meaning in the Book	Why I Think the Author Chose the Word
festivals	big parties that often happen at the same time every year	the word "festivals" makes me think of "festive," or fun
gold	a shiny yellow metal	"gold" makes me think of something special or valuable
carved	cut out or shaped from wood or stone	"carved" sounds more artistic than "cut"
decorations	things used to make something look good	"decorations" reminds me of a party
parades	fun marches often held at festival time	"parade" makes me think of a special event

Directions: Have children fill in the New Word Log using the words *festivals*, *gold*, *carved*, and other new words from *A World of Masks*.

Directions: Have children fill in the Text Connections Web for *A World of Masks*. Optional: Have children create a list of places and events where they have seen or worn masks.